Vegetarian Cooking
Around the World

Raita is a cool dish that is ideal to serve on hot summer days or as an accompaniment to spicy food. (Recipes on pages 38 and 39.)

Vegetarian Cooking

Around the World

PHOTOGRAPHS BY ROBERT L. AND DIANE WOLFE

easy menu
ethnic
cookbooks

Lerner Publications Company ▪ Minneapolis

Editor: Mary Winget

The page border for this book is based on a few of the ingredients that might be used in vegetarian recipes. The design includes grain, beets, carrots, mushrooms, olives, peas, squash, and tomatoes.

The photographs on the following pages are courtesy of: Ioansis Epaminondas, p. 30; FAO, p. 8; Jamaica Tourist Board, p. 35; John Kohnstamm, p. 38; L'Enc Matte, p. 15; Mia Lerner, p. 29; Jetty St. John, pp. 10, 13. Map and border by Laura Westlund.

This book is available in two editions:
Library binding by Lerner Publications Company
Soft cover by First Avenue Editions
241 First Avenue North
Minneapolis, MN   55401

Library of Congress Cataloging-in-Publication Data

Vegetarian cooking around the world / photographs by Robert L. and Diane Wolfe.
    p.   cm. — (Easy menu ethnic cookbooks)
    Includes index.
    Summary: A collection of meatless recipes from around the world, including Welsh rarebit from the United Kingdom, lentil soup from Spain, and curries from India.
    ISBN 0-8225-0927-X (lib. bdg.)
    ISBN 0-8225-9632-6 (pbk.)
    1. Vegetarian cookery—Juvenile literature 2. Cookery, International—Juvenile literature. [1. Vegetarian cookery. 2. Cookery, International.] I. Wolfe, Robert L., ill. II. Wolfe, Diane, ill. III. Series.
TX837.V4262 1992
641.5'636—dc20   91-45779
                                                        CIP
                                                        AC

Manufactured in the United States of America

  2   3   4   5   6   97   96   95   94   93

Polish people eat a variety of soups including this rich fruit soup, made with plums and rhubarb. It can be served hot or cold. (Recipe on page 42.)

CONTENTS

INTRODUCTION

Vegetarian meals are as good to eat as they are good for you, and they offer almost endless variety. In both the East and the West, vegetarian practices vary. Vegetarianism is the practice of not eating meat, fish, or poultry. Some vegetarians, called vegans (VEE-gans), also exclude from their diets eggs, milk, and other foods that come from animals. Others who consider themselves vegetarian eliminate red meat from their diets but continue to eat poultry or fish or both.

Attitudes about protein and meat-centered meals often stem from the land and culture in which people live. People get used to eating certain foods and avoiding others. In sharp contrast to the United States, Canada, Australia and Europe, where most people eat meat, in India the majority are vegetarian. In many parts of the world—regions of Africa, China, and the Middle East, for example—meat often is an unaffordable luxury for the average person. This book provides an introduction to vegetarian cooking. Many of the recipes include dairy products.

Why Vegetarianism?

People become vegetarians for many reasons. For some people, eating, or at least the type of food they eat, raises ethical issues. Some people believe that it is wrong to kill animals so that human beings can eat meat. Others believe it is unhealthy to eat meat. Certain religious groups, such as the Hindus, practice vegetarianism as part of their religion. Still others believe that the earth's ability to produce enough food to feed the world is limited. When you look at the world as a whole, good agricultural land is scarce, and a large portion of our limited agricultural resources is used to grow grain that will be fed to cattle. Some people believe it would make better sense to use that land to grow food that could be used for human consumption.

An Indian woman is preparing *chapati*—flat wheat bread—on an improved, smokeless stove. (Recipe on page 20.)

Is Meat Necessary for Good Health?

Children need a certain amount of protein in their diets in order to grow properly, and everyone needs protein to remain healthy. Although it is expensive to produce, meat is an excellent source of protein. But it is not the only source. Fruits, vegetables, grains, legumes (plants that grow seeds within pods, such as beans, peas, and lentils), and dairy products also provide protein. Eating plant foods in certain combinations during the same meal often produces more protein than if the same foods were eaten by themselves. Rice and beans, for example, provide complete protein when eaten together, but not when eaten separately. Plant foods also supply many vitamins and minerals, and they are low in fat and contain no cholesterol.

Planning the Menu

Although traditional meals in many Western countries are centered around meat served as a main course, vegetarian meals often consist of two or three courses of equal importance. Some vegetarian meals, however, do have a main course. Planning a meatless menu offers great flexibility. You can serve a meal around soup, bread, and salad or a casserole made with two or three vegetables. Different combinations of sauces provide a change of pace, and they can add zest and contrast to an otherwise simple meal.

When planning a vegetarian menu, you might want to consider the seasons of the year. Serve a hot, hearty soup on a cold winter night and perhaps a cold fruit soup on a warm summer evening. Although fresh produce can be flown in at all times of the year from almost any place in the world, certain fruits and vegetables are more readily available and are at their peak during particular seasons—crisp spears of asparagus in the spring, ripe corn and tomatoes in the summer. Take advantage of the variety.

Add an international flair to seasonal contrasts and the opportunities for tasty, interesting, vegetarian meals are multiplied. The recipes in this book are a sampling from around the world. Sixteen countries are represented, so use your imagination and savour some of the world's culinary treasures. Experience the world via your palate.

During the summer months, this Norwegian family prefers eating their evening meal outdoors. One of the dishes is called *pytti panna*, or "bits and pieces," made from potatoes, onions, and any other vegetables that happen to be in the refrigerator.

BEFORE YOU BEGIN

Cooking any dish, plain or fancy, is easier and more fun if you are familiar with its ingredients. The international dishes in this book make use of some ingredients you may not know. You should also be familiar with the special terms that will be used in these recipes. Therefore, *before* you start cooking any of the dishes in this book, study the following "dictionary" of special ingredients and terms very carefully. Then read through the recipe you want to try from beginning to end.

Now you are ready to shop for ingredients and to organize the cookware you will need. Once you have assembled everything, you can begin to cook. It is also very important to read *The Careful Cook* on page 44 before you start. Following these rules will make your cooking experience safe, fun, and easy.

COOKING UTENSILS

colander – A bowl with holes in the bottom and sides. It is used for draining liquid from a solid food.

kitchen parchment paper – A nonstick pan liner

kitchen shears – Scissors especially designed to snip herbs and cut a wide variety of foods

molinillo – A special wooden beater with rings of different sizes. It can be obtained in shops that specialize in Mexican goods.

rolling pin – A cylinder, usually of wood, used for rolling out pastry or dough

sieve – A bowl-shaped utensil made of wire mesh used to drain small, fine foods

slotted spoon – A spoon with small openings in the bowl. It is used to pick solid food out of a liquid.

spatula – A flat, thin utensil used to lift, toss, turn, or scoop up food

tongs – A utensil shaped either like tweezers or scissors with flat, blunt ends, used to grasp food

COOKING TERMS

beat – To stir rapidly in a circular motion

boil – To heat a liquid over a high heat until bubbles form and rise rapidly to the surface

broil – To cook directly under a heat source so that the side of the food facing the heat cooks rapidly

chop – To cut into small pieces

core – To remove the center part of a fruit or vegetable

cut in – A method of combining shortening (solid fat) and flour by using a pastry blender, a fork, or two knives. Cut the shortening into small pieces and mix them throughout the flour until mixture has a coarse, mealy consistency.

dollop – A small amount, about a teaspoonful, of a semiliquid ingredient such as whipped or sour cream

dust – To sprinkle the surface of something lightly with a substance, usually flour or sugar

grate – To cut into tiny pieces by rubbing the food against a grater

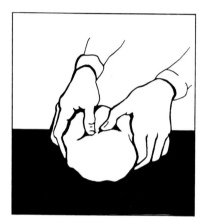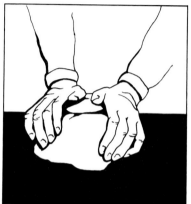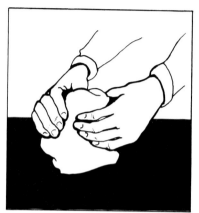

1. Form dough into a ball. 2. Press dough down with your palms. Then push it outward with the heel of your hand. 3. Fold and press dough over on itself. 4. Repeat Step 2, pressing dough down and pushing it outward.

knead – To work dough by pressing it with the palms, pushing it outward, and then pressing it over on itself

pinch – A very small amount, usually what you can pick up between your thumb and forefinger

preheat – To allow an oven to warm up to a certain temperature before putting food in it

sauté – To fry quickly over high heat in oil or fat, stirring or turning the food to prevent burning

sift – To put an ingredient, such as flour or sugar, through a sifter to break up any lumps

simmer – To cook over low heat in liquid kept just below the boiling point. Bubbles will occasionally rise to the surface.

stir-fry – To cook small pieces of meat, vegetables, poultry, or fish in a small amount of vegetable oil over high heat, stirring constantly.

SPECIAL INGREDIENTS

baking powder – A powder used as a leavening agent in baked goods to make the dough or batter lighter

basil – A rich, fragrant herb whose fresh or dried leaves are used in cooking

Bibb lettuce – A variety of lettuce that has a small head and dark green color

black-eyed peas – Small, tan peas with a large black spot from which they get their name

blue cheese – A sharp-tasting cheese with bluish green veins running through it

cardamom – A spice of the ginger family, used whole or ground, that has a rich aroma and gives food a sweet, cool taste

cayenne pepper – Dried red chilies ground to a fine powder

chickpeas – A type of dried pea with an irregular texture and a nutlike flavor; also called garbanzo beans

chilies – Small, hot red or green peppers

cinnamon – A spice made from the bark of

Andrea Johansen of Norway enjoys cooking with her mother.

a tree in the laurel family. It is available ground and in sticks.

coconut milk – The white, milky liquid extracted from coconut meat, used to give a coconut flavor to foods. It is available at oriental grocery stores.

coriander—An herb used as a flavoring and as a decorative garnish. Dried, powdered coriander is used in curries.

cornmeal—Coarsely ground dried corn

cornstarch—A fine, white starch made from corn, commonly used for thickening sauces and gravies

cumin—The seeds of an herb used whole or ground to give food a pungent, slightly hot flavor

curry powder—A blend of six or more spices that gives food a spicy flavor and a yellow hue

eggplant—A vegetable with shiny purple-black skin and yellow flesh

feta cheese—A crumbly, white cheese made from goat's milk

garlic—A bulbous herb whose distinctive flavor is used in many dishes. Each piece or bulb can be broken up into several small sections called cloves. Before chopping a clove of garlic, remove its papery skin.

garlic powder—Dehydrated garlic in a powder form

ginger root—The knobby, underground stem of ginger, a tropical plant, which gives a spicy-hot flavor when grated or thinly sliced and added to foods

kidney bean—A large, red bean named because of its shape

lentil—A flat, dried bean, or legume, that needs no soaking or precooking. Lentils are a good source of protein, vitamins, and minerals.

mung bean—A bean often used in oriental cooking that is available in oriental grocery stores

nutmeg—A fragrant spice, either whole or ground, that is often used in desserts

oat bran— The outer, protective covering of the oat grain

okra—The small, green pods of the okra plant; eaten as a vegetable

oregano—The dried leaves, whole or ground, of a rich and fragrant herb that is used as a seasoning in cooking

pimento—Small, sweet red chilies that come in cans or bottles and are often used to add color to food

plantain—A starchy fruit that looks like a banana and must be cooked before it is eaten

romaine lettuce—A lettuce with long, crisp, upright leaves

thyme—A fragrant herb used fresh or dry to season foods

turmeric—an aromatic East Indian herb

wheat bran—The outer layers of the wheat kernel

wheat germ—The heart or embryo of the wheat; it is sold toasted or sweetened and should be kept in the refrigerator.

yeast—An ingredient used in cooking to make bread rise and cause liquid to ferment

This market in Santiago, Chile, overflows with abundant fruits and vegetables.

AN INTERNATIONAL MENU

Below is a simplified menu for varied, international vegetarian meals. The ethnic names of the dishes are given, along with a guide on how to pronounce them. At least one alternate for each meal or course is provided.

ENGLISH NAME	ETHNIC NAME/ PRONUNCIATION GUIDE	COUNTRY
Beverages		
Mexican Hot Chocolate	Chocolate Mexicano	Mexico
Pineapple Fruit Cup		Australia
Breads and Staples		
Unleavened Whole Wheat Bread	Chapati (chuh-PAH-tee)	India
Deep-fried Whole Wheat Cakes	Puri (POO-ree)	India
Rice Pancakes		Kenya
Rye Bread	Rzhanoi Khleb (r'zhah-NOY HLEB)	Russia
Breakfast		
Fruit Muesli		Australia
Fresh Fruit Salad		Australia
Mushrooms on Toast		England

Lunch

Mixed Green Salad	Ensalada Mixta (ehn-sah-LAH-dah MEEX-tah)	Chile
Lentil Soup Madrid Style	Sopa de Lentejas Madrileña (SOH-pah day len-TAY-hahs mah-dray-LAY-nyah)	Spain
Bisignano Spinach	Spinaci Bisignano (speen-AH-chee bee-zee-NYAH-noh)	Italy
Stuffed Tomatoes with Feta Cheese	Domátes mé Féta (doh-MAH-tehs meh FEH-tah)	Greece

Dinner

Akkra		Jamaica
Rice and Peas		Trinidad/Tobago
Johnny Cakes		Caribbean Islands
Cornmeal Coo-coo		Barbados
Curried Chickpeas	Channa Dal (CHUHN-uh dahl)	India
Yogurt and Bananas	Kela ka Raita (KEE-lah kah RI-tah)	India
Yogurt with Cucumber and Tomato	Kheera-Tamatar Raita (KEER-ah tuh-MAH-tuhr RI-tah)	India
Choroko Sauce		Uganda
Groundnut Sauce		East and West Africa

Dessert

Plum and Rhubarb Soup		Poland
Anzac Biscuits		Australia

Hot chocolate flavored with cinnamon is a favorite breakfast beverage in Mexico. A *molinillo* is in the foreground.

BEVERAGES

Mexican Hot Chocolate/ *Chocolate Mexicano* Mexico

Recipe by Rosa Coronado

Stores that sell Mexican foods usually carry this special chocolate. It comes in cakes or tablets and contains sugar and cinnamon. Sweet cooking chocolate can also be used.

2 3-ounce cakes or tablets of Mexican chocolate or 6 ounces of sweet cooking chocolate
6 cups milk
1½ teaspoons cinnamon (if using cooking chocolate)

1. Combine all ingredients in a saucepan and cook over low heat. Stir constantly until chocolate has melted and mixture is blended.

2. With a *molinillo* (moh-lee-NEE-yoh, see page 11) or hand eggbeater, beat chocolate to a froth just before serving.

Serves 4

Pineapple Fruit Cup Australia

Recipe by Elizabeth Germaine and Ann L. Burckhardt

Australian familes serve a refreshing fruit drink like this for celebrations or on a hot afternoon.

4 cups pineapple juice
2 cups apricot nectar
1 cup orange juice
1 quart lemon-lime soda or club soda
1 quart ginger ale
1 apple
4 ounces candied cherries (optional)
  mint sprigs for garnish (optional)

1. Chill fruit juice and bottles of soda and ginger ale ahead of time.
2. Peel, core, and finely chop the apple.
3. With kitchen shears, cut candied

This delicious punch is most attractive when served in a clear pitcher and glass.

cherries into quarters.
4. Measure the pineapple juice, apricot nectar, and orange juice into a large pitcher or 1-gallon jug. Add chopped apple and cherries. Stir to mix well.
5. Add the soda and ginger ale just before serving. Pour into glasses filled with ice cubes and garnish with a sprig of mint.

Makes 10 to 12 servings

Russian rye bread is always a treat.

BREADS AND STAPLES

What we think of as breads and staples varies tremendously from country to country. Some of the breads featured here are very different from the plump, crusty loaves that are familiar to Westerners. Most Indian bread, for example, has no leavening agent like yeast, so it does not rise when it is cooked. *Chapati*, the most popular kind of Indian bread, is a flat, pancake-shaped bread that looks something like a Mexican tortilla. Like tortillas, chapati is cooked on a very hot, ungreased griddle. Chapati are also eaten in Kenya, Tanzania, and Uganda—countries in Africa. Russia is known the world over for its rye bread. The recipe given here makes a delicious, dense loaf that is well worth the time and the effort it takes to make it.

Unleavened Whole Wheat Bread/*Chapati*
India, Kenya, Tanzania, Uganda

Recipe by Vijay Madavan

2½ cups whole wheat flour
2 tablespoons butter or margarine
1 teaspoon salt
1 cup lukewarm water

1. Put 2 cups flour into a large mixing bowl.
2. Cut butter into small pieces. Make a hollow in the center of the flour and add butter. Rub butter into flour with your fingertips until mixture looks like large bread crumbs.

3. Mix salt into water. Add enough water, a little at a time, to flour mixture to make a firm (but not stiff) dough.

4. Knead dough in bowl for about 5 or 10 minutes. Cover bowl with a damp cloth and let stand at room temperature for at least 1 hour.

5. Divide dough into 1½-inch pieces, and roll each piece into a smooth ball.

6. Sprinkle remaining ½ cup flour onto a flat surface. With a rolling pin, roll out each ball until it resembles a thin pancake.

7. Heat a heavy skillet or griddle over medium-high heat. Place one *chapati* in the center. When small brown spots appear and the edges begin to curl up (in about 1 minute), turn the *chapati* over with a spatula. Cook *chapati* for about 2 minutes or until small brown spots appear. Wrap the cooked *chapati* in a towel to keep them warm.

8. Brush cooked *chapati* with melted butter and serve warm.

Makes 12 to 15 chapati

Deep-Fried Whole Wheat Cakes/*Puri*
India

Recipe by Vijay Madavan

whole wheat dough (recipe on p. 20)

1. Divide dough into pieces about the size of walnuts, and roll each piece into a smooth ball with your hands.

2. Sprinkle ½ cup flour on a flat surface. With a rolling pin, roll balls into thin rounds.

3. In a large skillet, heat oil over medium-high heat. Carefully place each *puri* in oil, one at a time. Using a spatula, carefully splash oil onto the *puri* while frying. This will make the *puri* puff up and will cook the top side. Fry each *puri* about 2 minutes or until golden brown on both sides.

4. Remove the *puri* from skillet, drain on paper towels, and serve immediately.

Makes 15 to 20 puri

Rice Pancakes
Kenya

Recipe by Constance Nabwire and
Bertha Vining Montgomery

*The addition of yeast makes these
pancakes light and airy. If the yeast does
not start to foam after about 5 minutes in
warm water, throw it out and try again with
new yeast.*

1 teaspoon active dry yeast
½ to 1 cup warm water (105 to 115°F)
1 cup sugar
2¾ cups rice flour
¼ teaspoon ground cardamom
¼ cup canned coconut milk
½ cup vegetable oil

1. In a small bowl, dissolve yeast in ½ cup warm water. Add a pinch of sugar and set aside in a warm place for about 5 minutes or until yeast mixture foams.
2. In a large bowl, combine sugar, flour, and cardamom. Add coconut milk and yeast mixture and stir. Mixture should have the consistency of pancake batter. If too thick, stir in water little by little until batter runs slowly from spoon.
3. Cover bowl with a towel (not terry cloth) and set aside in a warm place for about 1 hour or until mixture nearly doubles in size.
4. Heat 1 tablespoon oil over medium-high heat for 1 minute.
5. Pour ½ cup of batter into pan and spread with a spoon to form a pancake about the size of a saucer. Cover pan and cook for 1 to 2 minutes or until golden brown on bottom. Sprinkle pancake with a few drops of oil and turn over with a spatula. Cover and cook for another 1 to 2 minutes or until golden brown on other side. Repeat with remaining batter, adding more oil when necessary.
6. Serve hot.

Makes about 10 pancakes

Rye Bread/
Rzhanoi Khleb
Russia

Recipe by Gregory and Rita Plotkin

The secret to making good rye bread is not to add too much flour and to be patient enough to let the bread rise fully.

**2 packages active dry yeast
    (4½ teaspoons)
1 cup warm water (105 to 115°F)
⅓ cup dark corn syrup
4½ to 5½ cups dark rye flour
2 teaspoons salt**

1. In a large bowl, dissolve yeast in 1 cup warm water. Stir in corn syrup and set aside for 5 minutes until yeast mixture foams. If after 5 minutes yeast mixture has not started to foam, the water is too cold or too hot or the yeast is too old. Discard the yeast mixture and try again.
2. Add 2½ cups flour to the yeast mixture, a little at a time, and beat with a spoon until smooth. Stir in salt.
3. Set bowl in a warm place, cover with a cloth towel (not terry cloth), and let rise for 30 minutes.
4. Add 2 to 3 more cups flour, a half cup at a time, stirring after each addition. When dough becomes difficult to stir, turn out onto a floured surface and knead in flour with your hands until dough is stiff but still slightly sticky. Form dough into a ball.
5. Wash and dry bowl. Place dough in bowl, cover with a cloth towel, and set in a warm place. Let rise for 2½ to 3 hours or until dough almost doubles.
6. Turn dough out onto floured surface and, with floured hands, form into a loaf. Place loaf in a well-greased 9- by 5-inch baking pan, cover tightly with plastic wrap, and return to warm place to rise for 1 hour.
7. Preheat oven to 350°.
8. Bake for 30 to 35 minutes. (Bread will not brown much).

Makes 1 loaf

Muesli and fresh fruit salad served with toast and a beverage is a popular breakfast in Australia. *Vegemite* (the dark substance in the center) is often spread on toast.

BREAKFAST

Fruit Muesli
Australia

Recipe by Elizabeth Germaine and Ann L. Burckhardt

⅔ cup dried apricots
½ cup golden raisins
½ cup quick-cooking rolled oats
¼ cup oat bran or wheat germ
¼ cup wheat bran
2 tablespoons brown sugar
⅓ cup chopped walnuts or almonds

1. Cut the apricots into little pieces.
2. Measure the raisins, rolled oats, oat bran or wheat germ, wheat bran, and brown sugar into a mixing bowl. Add the apricots and nuts and toss gently.
3. Place in a container with a tight-fitting lid so the mixture will remain fresh.
4. Serve in a cereal bowl with milk, cream, or plain yogurt. Bananas, apples, or berries make an excellent topping.

Makes 8 (⅓ cup) servings

Fresh Fruit Salad
Australia

Recipe by Elizabeth Germaine and
Ann L. Burckhardt

*The beauty of fruit salad is that you can
use your imagination! It can be made with
almost any combination of fruits available.
In Australia, passion fruit is a common ingredient. Select three or four of your favorites.*

1 apple
1 orange
1 pear
  small bunch of grapes
2 tablespoon sugar (optional)

1. Wash the fruit carefully, then peel, core,
and remove the stone or pit, if there is one.
Cut the fruit into small chunks or bite-
sized pieces.
2. Combine the fruit in a bowl. Add 2 tablespoons of sugar (optional). Stir the fruit
gently, being careful not to bruise or mash
it. Cover and chill until ready to serve.

Serves 3 to 4

Mushrooms on Toast
England

Recipe by Barbara W. Hill

½ pound fresh mushrooms
2 tablespoons butter
  salt and pepper
1 tablespoon cornstarch
1 cup milk
4 slices buttered toast

1. Wash mushrooms and drain on a paper
towel. Cut into quarters.
2. Melt butter in a frying pan. Add mushrooms and salt and pepper to taste. Sauté
until soft.
3. In a cup, mix cornstarch with a little of
the milk to make a smooth, thin paste.
Then add rest of milk and stir until mixture is free of lumps.
4. Slowly add milk mixture to mushrooms
in the pan, stirring constantly. Cook over
low heat for 1 minute.
5. Pour mixture over toast and serve.

Serves 4

LUNCH

Mixed Green Salad/ *Ensalada Mixta* Chile

Recipe by Helga Parnell

1 head Bibb lettuce
1 head romaine lettuce
4 ripe olives (optional)
4 cherry tomatoes, quartered (optional)
¼ cup blue cheese, crumbled (optional)

1. Arrange lettuce in salad bowl.
2. Top with a dressing of your choice and toss to coat leaves.
3. Garnish with olives, tomatoes, and cheese.

Serves 6

Lentil Soup Madrid Style/*Sopa de Lentejas Madrileña* Spain

Recipe by Rebecca Christian

1 large onion, chopped
1 canned whole pimento, drained and chopped
1 green pepper, cleaned out and chopped
4 tablespoons olive oil
2 tablespoons all-purpose flour
1 16-ounce can (2 cups) tomatoes, cut up with a spoon
3 carrots, peeled and chopped
2 cups lentils (do not presoak)
1 tablespoon salt
8 cups water

1. In a large kettle, cook onion, pimento, and green pepper in olive oil until soft.
2. Stir in flour. Then add tomatoes, carrots, lentils, salt, and water. Cover and simmer over very low heat for about 2 hours.

Serves 12

Sopa de lentejas Madrileña is a popular Spanish soup that is especially appealing in cool weather.

Bisignano spinach makes a nutritious vegetarian main dish.

Bisignano Spinach/
Spinaci Bisignano
Italy

Recipe by Alphonse Bisignano

2 10-ounce packages frozen chopped spinach, cooked, or 1½ pounds fresh spinach, cooked and finely chopped
1 16-ounce carton (2 cups) ricotta or cottage cheese

1 cup bread crumbs or packaged herb stuffing
2 eggs, lightly beaten
¼ cup sliced fresh mushrooms or canned mushrooms, drained
½ cup chopped green pepper
8 ounces (1 cup) sour cream
½ cup spaghetti sauce, canned or homemade
1 pound mozzarella cheese, sliced
1 teaspoon basil
½ cup grated Parmesan cheese

1. Preheat the oven to 350°.
2. In a large bowl, combine spinach, ricotta or cottage cheese, bread crumbs, eggs, mushrooms, and green pepper.
3. Pour mixture into a buttered 9- by 13-inch baking dish and spread sour cream on top.
4. Pour on a layer of spaghetti sauce. Cover with a layer of mozzarella cheese slices.
5. Spread remaining spaghetti sauce over cheese slices. Sprinkle with basil and Parmesan cheese.
6. Bake for 30 minutes.

Serves 6 to 8

In Venice, Italy, many of the streets are actually canals, and transportation is by gondola (*above*) or powerboat.

Stuffed Tomatoes with Feta Cheese/
Domátes mé Féta
Greece

Recipe by Lynne W. Villios

Fine, fresh vegetables are found throughout Greece. For this recipe, it is important to use the reddest, ripest tomatoes available.

4 ripe, medium tomatoes
2 tablespoons finely chopped scallions
2 tablespoons finely chopped fresh
    parsley
½ cup (about 3 ounces) finely
    crumbled feta cheese
¼ cup bread crumbs
3 tablespoons olive oil

1. Carefully cut tops off tomatoes. Using a spoon, carefully scoop out pulp and seeds. Save pulp and discard seeds.
2. Coarsely chop the tomato pulp.
3. Preheat oven to 350°.
4. In a small bowl, combine tomato pulp with scallions, parsley, feta cheese, bread crumbs, and olive oil.
5. Spoon mixture into the hollowed-out tomatoes. Place tomatoes right side up in an 8- by 8-inch baking pan and bake 15 minutes.
6. Serve stuffed tomatoes steaming hot.

Serves 4

The ruins of the Erechtheion, a temple built in 395 B.C., is on a hill called the Acropolis in Athens, Greece.

DINNER

Caribbean Style

These mild-flavored dishes round out a Caribbean meal. Akkra can be eaten as an appetizer, and rice and peas is hearty enough to serve alone for lunch.

Akkra
Jamaica

Recipe by Cheryl Davidson Kaufman

Akkra is sometimes made with salt fish instead of ground peas.

2 cups dried black-eyed peas
6 chilies
⅓ cup water
vegetable oil for frying

1. Place peas in a large saucepan and cover with water. Let soak overnight.

2. Rub peas together between your palms to remove skins. Skins will float to top of water and can be skimmed off. Let peas soak for another 2 hours after skins are removed.

3. Place peas in a blender, 1 cup at a time, and blend about 20 seconds until smooth. Remove ground peas from blender, place in a large bowl.

4. Cut chilies in half and remove stems and seeds. Place in blender and blend about 20 seconds.

5. Add ground chilies to peas and stir. If mixture is dry, stir in water, little by little, until pasty. Beat with a spoon until light and fluffy.

6. Pour 1 inch of oil into a large frying pan and heat for 4 or 5 minutes over medium-high heat. Carefully drop rounded tablespoons of pea mixture into oil and fry 2 to 3 minutes per side or until golden brown. Remove from oil with slotted spoon and drain on paper towels.

Serves 6

Rice and Peas
Trinidad, Tobago, and Jamaica

Recipe by Cheryl Davidson Kaufman

When I was growing up, no Sunday dinner at my house was complete without rice and peas. In the Caribbean, beans are called peas.

1 cup dried red kidney beans
4 cups coconut milk
1 clove garlic, peeled and chopped, or
**   1 teaspoon garlic powder**
2 green onions
3 sprigs fresh thyme or ¼ teaspoon
**   dried thyme**
1 teaspoon salt
½ teaspoon black pepper
3 cups water
3 cups uncooked long-grain white rice

1. Place beans in a colander and rinse well with cold water.
2. In a large saucepan, combine beans, coconut milk, and garlic. Bring to a boil over high heat. Reduce heat to low and cover, leaving cover slightly ajar. Simmer for about 1½ hours or until beans are tender. Do not overcook.
3. Add green onions, thyme, salt, black pepper, 3 cups water, and rice. Bring to a boil over high heat. Reduce heat to low and cover tightly, placing a paper towel between saucepan and lid. Simmer for 20 minutes.
4. Remove cover and paper towel, and stir gently with a fork. Rice grains should be separate and fluffy and water should be absorbed. If not done, cover and continue to cook, checking every 5 minutes until done.

Serves 6 to 8

These dishes make a Caribbean meal complete. Pictured are (*clockwise starting top left*) rice and peas, cornmeal coo-coo, johnny cakes, and akkra.

Johnny Cakes All Islands

Recipe by Cheryl Davidson Kaufman

These fried biscuits are called bakes in Trinidad and Tobago and johnny cakes on the other islands.

2 cups all-purpose flour
½ teaspoon salt
1 teaspoon baking powder
1 tablespoon plus 2 teaspoons butter
**   or margarine, softened**
¼ cup cold water
**   vegetable oil for frying**

1. Sift flour, salt, and baking powder together into a large bowl.
2. With clean hands, rub butter into flour mixture until mixture is grainy. Stir in water, little by little, until dough can be formed into a ball but is not sticky.
3. Place dough on a clean, flat surface that has been dusted with flour. Dust a rolling pin with flour and roll out dough to about ¼ inch thickness. Dip the rim of a glass in flour and cut dough into circles. Repeat with remaining dough until all dough has been used up.
4. Pour ¼ inch oil into medium frying pan and heat over medium-high heat for 4 or 5 minutes.
5. Fry biscuits a few at a time for 3 or 4 minutes per side or until golden brown. Remove with slotted spoon and drain on paper towels.

Makes 10 to 12 biscuits

Cornmeal Coo-coo Barbados

Recipe by Cheryl Davidson Kaufman

This recipe calls for okra, a small, green vegetable that was brought to the Caribbean from West Africa.

Fruits and vegetables are often sold at outdoor stalls in Jamaica.

3 teaspoons butter or margarine
1 medium onion, peeled and chopped
2 cups water
1 10-ounce package frozen okra, thawed
1 cup yellow cornmeal

1. In a small frying pan, melt 1 tablespoon butter over medium heat. Add onions and sauté until transparent. Remove from heat and set aside.
2. In a large saucepan, bring 2 cups water to a boil over high heat. Add okra and reduce heat to low.
3. Slowly pour cornmeal into water while stirring constantly. Cook for 7 or 8 minutes, stirring constantly, until mixture begins to thicken.
4. Add remaining butter and onions and stir. Pour into shallow serving dish and smooth the top with a knife. Serve immediately.

Serves 6

DAL
India

Dal *is the Hindi word for pulses, those versatile beans, lentils, and peas that are such an important part of the Indian diet. Most Indians have some kind of* dal *at almost every meal. Eaten with a starchy food like bread or rice and a milk product such as yogurt, they form the basis of a well-balanced diet. On the following page is a recipe for a hearty dish of chickpeas, or* channa dal *in Hindi. In preparing any* dal, *be sure to examine the pulses for small stones, twigs, and other inedible objects before cooking them.*

Channa dal **can be teamed with yogurt and** *chapati* **(recipe on page 20) to make a simple but nourishing meal.**

Curried Chickpeas/
Channa Dal
India

Recipe by Vijay Madavan

1½ **cups (12 ounces) chickpeas, washed**
   and drained
5 **cups water**
1 **teaspoon ground tumeric**
½ **teaspoon ground cumin**
1 **teaspoon ground coriander**
½ **teaspoon cayenne pepper (optional)**
3 **tablespoons butter or margarine**
1 **teaspoon cumin seed**
1 **medium onion, chopped**
1 **clove garlic, chopped**
1 **tablespoon grated fresh ginger**
2 **tablespoons chopped fresh coriander**
   leaves

1. Put chickpeas in a bowl. Add enough cold water to cover and soak overnight.
2. To cook, drain chickpeas. Place chickpeas, water, tumeric, cumin, coriander, and cayenne in a heavy saucepan and bring to a boil over medium-high heat. Reduce heat to low, cover pan, and simmer for about 1 hour.
3. In a large saucepan, melt butter over medium heat. Add cumin seed and cook for 1 minute. Add the onion, garlic, and ginger and cook for about 5 minutes, stirring frequently, or until onion turns golden brown.
4. Add chickpeas and cooking liquid to onion mixture. Turn heat to high and bring to a boil, stirring constantly. Cover pan, reduce heat to low, and simmer 30 minutes or until chickpeas are tender but not mushy. Mix well.
5. Place chickpeas in a serving dish and sprinkle with chopped coriander leaves.

Serves 6 to 8

RAITA
India

As an accompaniment to the spicy flavor of an Indian meal, nothing could be better than a raita, *a cool and crunchy combination of yogurt with vegetables, fruits, and various seasonings. Indian cooks usually make their own yogurt out of water-buffalo milk. You can make yogurt out of cow's milk or use unflavored yogurt from the supermarket.*

Yogurt and Bananas/
Kela ka Raita
India

Recipe by Vijay Madavan

1½ cups (12 ounces) plain yogurt
 2 large bananas, peeled and sliced
 ¼ cup flaked coconut
 1 green chili, finely chopped
 1 teaspoon lemon juice
 ¼ teaspoon ground coriander
 ¼ teaspoon cinnamon
 ¼ teaspoon salt
 1 teaspoon finely chopped fresh
   coriander leaves

1. In a medium mixing bowl, beat yogurt until smooth. Stir in bananas, coconut, chili, lemon juice, coriander, cinnamon, and salt. Cover bowl and chill at least 1 hour.
2. Just before serving, sprinkle coriander leaves over raita.

Serves 4

Yogurt with Cucumber and Tomato/ *Kheera-Tamatar Raita* India

Recipe by Vijay Madavan

This recipe can also be used as a dip to serve with fresh, raw vegetables or as a dressing on lettuce leaves garnished with tomato wedges.

1 medium tomato
1 medium cucumber, peeled
2 cups (16 ounces) plain yogurt
1 small onion, chopped
3 tablespoons chopped fresh coriander
    or parsley
½ teaspoon salt
½ teaspoon black pepper
    dash of cayenne pepper (optional)

1. Cut tomato in half and remove seeds. Chop tomato into small pieces.
2. Chop cucumber into small pieces.
3. In a bowl, beat yogurt until smooth. Combine yogurt with remaining ingredients and mix well.
4. Cover bowl and chill at least 1 hour before serving.

Serves 4

Wearing brightly colored *saris*, these women shop for the day's food.

Choroko Sauce Uganda

Recipe by Constance Nabwire and Bertha Vining Montgomery

Although the flavor will be different, choroko sauce can also be made with split peas.

1½ **cups dried Shirakiku brand mung beans**
 2 **tablespoons vegetable oil**
 3 **medium tomatoes, cut into bite-sized pieces**
 1 **large onion, peeled and chopped**
 3 **or 4 cloves garlic, peeled and crushed**
 ½ **teaspoon seasoned salt**
   dash salt
   dash black pepper
 ½ **cup water**

1. Place beans in a medium bowl and cover with water. Let soak overnight.
2. Drain beans in a colander.
3. Fill a medium saucepan half full of water and bring to a boil over high heat. Add beans and cook for 1 to 1½ hours or until tender.
4. Drain beans in a colander and place in a medium bowl. Mash well with a fork.
5. In a large frying pan, heat oil over medium heat for 1 minute.
6. Add tomatoes, onions, and garlic and sauté until onions are transparent.
7. Add mashed beans, seasoned salt, salt, black pepper, and ½ cup water and simmer for 15 to 20 minutes. Serve over rice or with chapatis.

Serves 4 to 6

Groundnut Sauce East and West Africa

Recipe by Constance Nabwire and Bertha Vining Montgomery

This sauce is made from groundnuts, better known in some countries as peanuts. This recipe works best if made with natural peanut butter with no sugar added.

2 tablespoons vegetable oil
1 medium onion, peeled and chopped
2 medium tomatoes, cut into bite-sized
   pieces
1 small eggplant, with or without peel,
   cut into bite-sized pieces
½ cup smooth peanut butter
¼ cup water

1. In a large frying pan, heat oil over medium heat for 1 minute. Add onions and sauté until transparent.
2. Add tomatoes and cook for 5 minutes. Add eggplant and cook for 5 minutes more.
3. In a small bowl, combine peanut butter and ¼ cup water and stir to make a paste. Add to tomato mixture and stir well.
4. Reduce heat to medium-low and simmer, uncovered, for 10 minutes or until eggplant is tender.
5. Serve with rice, potatoes, sweet potatoes, or plantains.

Serves 4 to 6

Flavorful groundnut sauce (*front*) and choroko sauce (*back*) are rich in protein. They can be served with *chapati* (recipe on page 20) or over rice.

DESSERT

Plum and Rhubarb Soup
Poland

Recipe by Danuta Zamojska-Hutchins

This delicious fruit soup is easy to make and can be eaten either hot at the beginning of a meal or cold for dessert.

Dried, pitted prunes can be used instead of plums, and tart green apples can be substituted for rhubarb. If you use apples, peel and core them. If you use prunes, cover them with water and soak overnight. The liquid can then be used in the soup.

½ pound plums or pitted, dried prunes
½ pound rhubarb or tart green apples
6 cups water
3 or 4 whole cloves
1 small stick cinnamon
¼ cup sugar
2 tablespoons all-purpose flour or
** cornstarch**
½ cup sour cream

1. Wash fruit. Remove pits and stems from plums. Remove ends and tops of rhubarb. Chop fruit into chunks.
2. Combine fruit, water, cloves, cinnamon, and sugar in a large kettle. Bring to a boil, then cover, reduce heat, and simmer for 10 to 15 minutes.
3. Remove cloves and cinnamon with a slotted spoon and discard.
4. Remove half of fruit with slotted spoon and mash with a fork.
5. In a cup, add ¼ cup cold water to flour or cornstarch, a little at a time, to make a thick paste.
6. Add paste to the mashed fruit, then return fruit to kettle and bring to a boil.
7. As soon as soup begins to boil, remove from heat and let stand for 3 or 4 minutes.
8. Serve soup hot or cold with dollops of sour cream on top.

Serves 6 to 8

Anzac biscuits are favorites at teatime in Australia.

Anzac Biscuits
Australia

Recipe by Elizabeth Germaine and
Ann L. Burckhardt

*These cookies were named for the Australia
and New Zealand Army Corps (ANZAC),
which fought in World War I.*

1 **cup rolled oats**
¾ **cup unsweetened shredded coconut**
¾ **cup all-purpose flour**
1 **cup sugar**
½ **cup butter or margarine**
1 **tablespoon honey or light corn syrup**

3 **tablespoons boiling water**
1½ **teaspoons baking soda**
   kitchen parchment paper or
   heavy-duty aluminum foil

1. Measure the oats, coconut, flour, and
sugar into a medium-sized mixing bowl;
toss to mix.
2. Melt butter and honey or corn syrup in
a small pan over medium-low heat.
3. Pour boiling water over baking soda and
stir to dissolve. Add to the melted butter
mixture.
4. Pour the butter mixture over the mixed
dry ingredients; mix well.
5. Heat oven to 300°. Cover 2 baking sheets
with kitchen parchment paper or heavy-
duty aluminum foil (dull side up).
6. Drop teaspoonfuls of dough 2 inches
apart onto prepared baking sheets.
7. Bake 10 to 12 minutes, until crisp and
golden brown.
8. Cool cookies on baking sheet 1 to 2
minutes, then remove with a spatula and
cool on wire racks. When cool, store in
an airtight container.
Makes about 4 dozen cookies

THE CAREFUL COOK

Whenever you cook, there are certain safety rules you must always keep in mind. Even experienced cooks follow these rules when they are in the kitchen.

1. Always wash your hands before handling food.
2. Thoroughly wash all raw vegetables and fruits to remove dirt, chemicals, and insecticides.
3. Use a cutting board when cutting up vegetables and fruits. Don't cut them up in your hand! And be sure to cut in a direction *away* from you and your fingers.
4. Long hair or loose clothing can catch fire if brought near the burners of a stove. If you have long hair, tie it back before you start cooking.
5. Turn all pot handles away from you so that you will not catch your sleeves or jewelry on them. This is especially important when younger brothers and sisters are around. They could easily knock a pot off the stove and get burned.

6. Always use a pot holder to steady hot pots or to take pans out of the oven. Don't use a wet cloth on a hot pan because the steam it produces can burn you.
7. Lift the lid of a steaming pot with the opening away from you so that you will not get burned.
8. If you get burned, hold the burn under cold running water. Do not put grease or butter on it. Cold water helps to take the heat out, but grease or butter will only keep it in.
9. If grease or cooking oil catches fire, throw baking soda or salt at the bottom of the flame to put it out. (Water will *not* put out a grease fire.) Call for help, and try to turn all the stove burners to "off."

METRIC CONVERSION CHART

WHEN YOU KNOW		MULTIPLY BY	TO FIND	
MASS (weight)				
ounces	(oz)	28.0	grams	(g)
pounds	(lb)	0.45	kilograms	(kg)
VOLUME				
teaspoons	(tsp)	5.0	milliliters	(ml)
tablespoons	(Tbsp)	15.0	milliliters	
fluid ounces	(oz)	30.0	milliliters	
cup	(c)	0.24	liters	(l)
pint	(pt)	0.47	liters	
quart	(qt)	0.95	liters	
gallon	(gal)	3.8	liters	
TEMPERATURE				
Fahrenheit	(°F)	5/9 (after subtracting 32)	Celsius	(°C)

COMMON MEASURES AND THEIR EQUIVALENTS

3 teaspoons = 1 tablespoon

8 tablespoons = ½ cup

2 cups = 1 pint

2 pints = 1 quart

4 quarts = 1 gallon

16 ounces = 1 pound

INDEX

Stuffed tomatoes with feta cheese make a tasty lunch or an attractive side dish. (Recipe on page 30.)

easy menu ethnic cookbooks

Rice pancakes (*bottom*) and *chapati* (*top*) can be served with sauces or alone as a snack. *Chapati* are delicious with butter or sprinkled with sugar, and rice pancakes are often eaten with jam. (Recipes on pages 20-22.)